Author:
Jacqueline Morley studied English at
Oxford University. She has taught English and
History, and now works as a freelance writer.
She has written historical fiction and non-fiction
for children.

Artist:
David Antram was born in Brighton, England,
in 1958. He studied at Eastbourne College of Art
and then worked in advertising for fifteen years
before becoming a full-time artist. He has
illustrated many children's non-fiction books.

Series Creator:
David Salariya was born in Dundee, Scotland.
He has illustrated a wide range of books and has
created and designed many new series for
publishers both in the UK and overseas. In 1989,
he established The Salariya Book Company. He
lives in Brighton with his wife, illustrator Shirley
Willis, and their son Jonathan.

Editor: **Sophie Izod**

Published in Great Britain in 2006 by
Book House, an imprint of
The Salariya Book Company Ltd
25 Marlborough Place, Brighton BN1 1UB

Please visit the Salariya Book Company at:
www.salariya.com
www.book-house.co.uk

HB ISBN 1 905087 55 1
PB ISBN 1 905087 56 X

A catalogue record for this book is available
from the British Library.

Printed and bound in China.

Avoid working on the Great Wall of China!

Written by
Jacqueline Morley

Illustrated by
David Antram

Created and designed by
David Salariya

The Danger Zone

BOOK HOUSE

Contents

Introduction

Y ou're a poor farmer living in China around 215 BC. With plenty of things to worry about – bad weather, poor crops and big taxes to pay, you've barely noticed the political upheavals taking place around you recently. A few years ago, China as one nation did not exist. The land was divided between rival states who had been fighting each other for centuries. But now a really strong ruler from the state of Qin has emerged. He has united the country and called himself Qin Shihuangdi, which means 'First Great Emperor of China.' He is ruthless and cruel. No one dares to disobey his orders, and he does not care how many people die carrying them out. You are one of the unlucky thousands he sends to build a huge defensive wall 3000 kilometres long on China's northern border. It's still there today (although much restored and rebuilt) and is known as the Great Wall of China.

THE GREAT WALL

Yellow River

YELLOW SEA

Xiangyang

Yangtze River

	Lines of fortifications
	The Emperor's new roads
	The Emperor's canals
	Boundary of Qin Empire 221-206 BC

The First Great Emperor

The Emperor has "all-seeing eyes, the nose of a hornet, the voice of a jackal and the heart of a wolf." That's how one of his advisors described him (before fleeing for his life). You saw the Emperor once, and it's a fair description. He was driving along one of the many new highways he ordered built to speed communications and tighten his control. He has made everyone use the same currency, writing characters, weights and measures, and distance between their cart-wheels (so they can run in the same ruts). There are rules for everything.

How he rules:

HE'S BUILT a magnificent new capital, Xiangyang, and made the head-strong nobles hand in their swords, leave their lands, and live there under his watchful eye.

THROUGHOUT the land, government officials write him reports on strips of bamboo laced together and rolled up – there is no paper.

THE EMPEROR is a tireless worker. He weighs his pile of reports to make sure he's done his daily quota.

DISOBEYING him is most unwise. Punishments include beheading, being buried alive, and being cut-in-half at the waist.

6

Handy hint

Don't criticise the Emperor or you will never be promoted – if you survive at all!

Everlasting Rule

Build, build, build!

POOR PEOPLE everywhere are forced to work on the Emperor's projects – soldiers, convicts, slaves, and ordinary people just like you. You see large numbers of them being marched off to dig canals or to build new roads and fortifications. Your time will come.

The Emperor is very superstitious and terrified of dying. He hopes to cheat death by finding the 'elixir of life,' a magical substance that will make him immortal. He has sent expeditions far and wide to seek it, so far with no success. If this plan fails he has another one. He has 700,000 workers building a tomb containing a model of his kingdom, so that he will continue ruling in the next world. They are also making an army to guard it – over 8,000 life-size figures of men, horses, and chariots made from terracotta and buried underground.

UNDERGROUND TOMB. In the inner chamber of the Emperor's tomb, a dragon ferries his copper coffin across a model of his kingdom complete with gem-studded palaces and towers. The ceiling represents the star-filled sky, while below, the rivers of China, made in quicksilver, flow into a quicksilver ocean. (As described by a Chinese historian of c.100 BC. It has not been excavated.)

FROM THE TERRACOTTA ARMY: a general (left), an officer and his horse (above), and a kneeling crossbowman (his bow has not survived).

A Hard Life

DROUGHT AND FLOOD
Bad weather can ruin all your hopes. If no rain falls, your crops will shrivel. But if it does rain, the Yellow River may flood and drown them.

ike most of the Emperor's subjects, you live in the country and scrape a living from a small piece of land. It belongs to your father who's getting old now but still makes all the decisions and you must obey him. That is the duty of Chinese sons and daughters, no matter how old they are. You work every day of the year, but still it's hard to grow enough to feed the family – yourself, your parents and your sister – and to have anything left over to sell. Every year you pay tax to the Emperor, and this is calculated according to the size of your land, not the size of your crop. When the harvest is poor, there's nothing left once the tax has been paid. In order to eat and to buy seed for next year's crop you have to borrow money, and once you get into debt it is very hard to get out. Many poor farmers are ruined this way.

From bad to worse:

A You borrow money from a rich landowner to pay your debts.
B You have to sell animals and tools to pay him back.
C You can't work the farm without tools so you are forced to sell it to the landowner. You become his tenant, do all the work, and he keeps all the profit.
D The last straw – a conscription officer selects you to do forced labour.

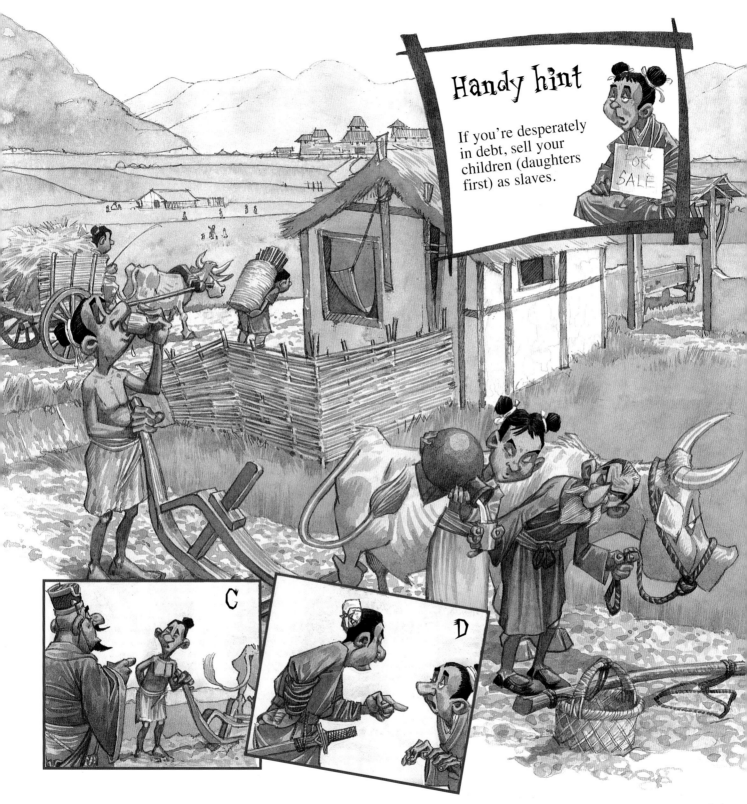

Handy hint

If you're desperately in debt, sell your children (daughters first) as slaves.

Old Duties and New Laws

You have been brought up to believe that family loyalty is the most important thing in life. Two-and-a-half centuries before your time, the great Chinese thinker and teacher, Confucius, emphasised this. You must offer food to the spirits of your ancestors so they will protect your family, because if they feel neglected they may harm them. Every home has a shrine to its family ancestors and the honour of worshipping them is handed on from father to son. But your new Emperor has introduced a very different duty – loyalty and total obedience to him. By law you must report all breaking of his rules, even if this means informing on members of your family. If you do not, you will be judged to be as guilty as they are. Most people feel very unhappy about these changes, but few dare to say so openly.

Old-style duties:

OBEY YOUR ELDERS A wife always obeys her husband, but she shows her parents-in-law even more respect, since they are older.

TRADITIONALLY all generations of a Chinese family live and eat together, and all belongings are shared among them.

A FATHER can beat his grown-up son, and even get him banished, with no appeal.

WIVES WITHOUT sons can adopt one (who must be a blood relation) because females cannot continue the tradition of ancestor worship.

Handy hint

Only give birth to sons. A daughter will be a big disappointment to your family.

New-style obedience to the law:

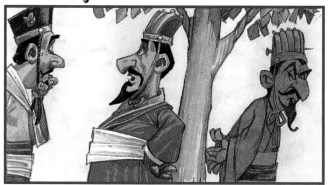

DENOUNCE YOUR NEIGHBOURS If you hear something the Emperor wouldn't like, it is your duty to report it or you will be blamed.

PERMITS AND PASSES To make a journey you need a permit from an official, so that he can report what you're up to.

The Burning of the Books

Some scholars who study the writings of past thinkers, have been brave enough to criticise the Emperor. They say he cannot rule exactly as he pleases, for books of wisdom explain that a ruler has duties towards his subjects as well as powers over them. The Emperor intends to stop this dangerous talk. He has ordered all books (except those on farming, medicine and soothsaying) to be handed in and burned on public bonfires. Anyone quoting books to criticise the Emperor will be put to death. Already over 460 leading scholars have been buried alive.

SEARCHING Soldiers are searching houses and gardens for hidden books. If they find any, the owner is executed on the spot.

BURYING BOOKS A terrified old scholar begs you to hide a box of his precious books by burying them in your field. He pays you well.

Handy hint

To preserve a well-loved book, learn it by heart.

CAUGHT! "I only did it for the money!" you plead when you are caught. You're sentenced to five years on the Great Wall.

BACK IN THE CELLS, you ask what the Great Wall is. "They call it the longest graveyard in the world," a fellow prisoner tells you.

Raiders from the North

You're going to China's northern border, where people live in terror of the Xiongnu, the wandering herdsmen from the steppes. Their animals provide their food, clothes and shelter, but for other needs they go trading or, more often, raiding. They are incredibly skilled horsemen, swooping out of nowhere, killing villagers and taking whatever they want. The Emperor has decided to build a huge wall to keep them out. It will run the length of his kingdom from east to west, linking some existing walls and going far beyond them. He wants it built fast and he doesn't care how many people die building it.

What you've heard about the Xiongnu:

HOUSING They don't live in houses like normal people but in round tents made of animal skins. Even their clothes are made from skin instead of cloth.

FOOD AND DRINK They eat and drink the most disgusting things. For instance, they drink milk and make cheese, which no Chinese person would dream of doing.

NO TASTE When Chinese diplomats brought them expensive gifts, they turned their noses up at the most delicious delicacies.

Attack!

Handy hint

Watch out at harvest time. While everyone is in the fields, the Xiongnu will raid the village.

NO STYLE They say silk trousers wear out if you ride in them for a week.

17

The Journey North

Branded, put in a convict's rough hemp robe, and chained to the next man, you're being marched to the Wall. From your home village in central China, this means a six-to-eight-week journey on foot. As you go further north, more and more lines of convicts pour in from side-roads, until the route is almost blocked with them. You have no idea where you are, you just stumble on exhausted. The guards don't care what state you're in as long as they get you to the Wall in the allotted time. Several people have collapsed and died.

The 6-8 week journey:

IN MANY PARTS the roads are terrible. You must clamber up slopes and wade through rivers with no bridges.

CROSSING DENSE forest is the worst, for it's well-known that demons live there. You are terrified.

SOMETIMES the road is just a wooden walkway, clinging to the side of a gorge.

Handy hint

Cheer up. At least you're not being executed like an official you pass on the road.

THE LAST STRETCH crosses desert wastes.

FINALLY you arrive at a military encampment by the Wall.

Walk faster!

19

The Emperor's Great Wall

WEAK POINTS in the wall, where rivers cross it, are guarded by especially large towers full of soldiers.

SMALLER TOWERS are closely set so that raiders storming the wall are never out of arrow range.

Your first thought on seeing the Wall is "A wall can't be that long!" And this is just the part they've built so far – it twists and turns like an enormous wriggling dragon, along the highest ridges of ground. It's guarding China from the wilderness beyond, where lawless people and cruel demons live. The towers are set at regular intervals along the Wall and manned by soldiers who are constantly on guard. General Meng T'ien, who is in charge of this great project, has put 300,000 troops to work on the Wall and just as importantly, on the roads to protect the supplies. You soon learn to watch for the arrival of the grain wagons. If they've had an accident or if their contents get stolen on the way here, you'll soon all be starving.

THE WALL'S AMAZING number of towers are explained differently by ordinary people. They say that the First Great Emperor galloped the whole length of the Wall on his magic flying horse, and wherever its hooves touched the Wall a tower sprang up.

Building the Wall

Under the whip, day in, day out, your work is endless, and no one cares if you are sick or dead. You build the Wall over mountains and across desert. In rocky areas you use stone, but in most places there isn't any suitable stone and the whole wall has to be made of pounded earth. When you're in one of the supply gangs, you dig earth, carry it to the site and tip it into a wooden frame. If you're in a frame gang you spread the earth out thinly, no more than 13 cm deep, and ram it down with pounders. When that layer is hard and dry, a new one goes on top. When the stack is high enough the frame is taken down and moved. It takes much sweat and many days to build a section 10 m tall and wide enough for five horsemen to ride side-by-side along its top.

SOAKED TO THE SKIN: Weather never puts a halt to work. You carry loads, haul logs, and pound earth in pouring rain.

SWELTERING HEAT: In blazing summer heat you hack through undergrowth to make a clearing for a new stretch of the Wall.

FREEZING COLD: Chilled to the bone in icy mountains, you cut through solid rock to make a level foundation for the Wall.

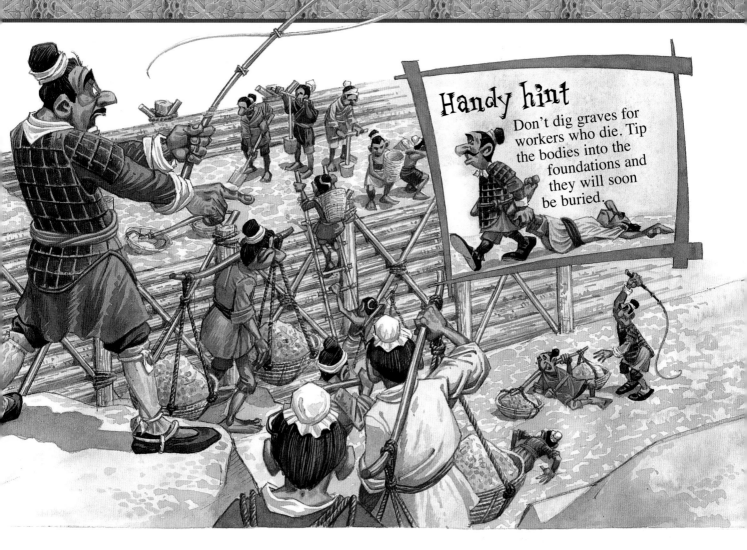

Handy hint

Don't dig graves for workers who die. Tip the bodies into the foundations and they will soon be buried.

WATCH YOUR STEP: No one cares about your safety. You stagger under heavy loads all day, often up dangerous slopes...

AN EMPTY STOMACH: Only boiled millet again for supper! The army grows food locally now but there is not always enough to go round.

ALL IN A DAY'S WORK: After working every hour of daylight, you fall asleep exhausted on your patch of straw, inside a crowded tent.

Along the Watch Tower

After three years of hard labour, your sentence has been commuted to military service and you're stationed on a watch tower along the Wall you helped build! Army life is tough with cramped quarters, iron discipline, and constant inspections by the company commander. If anything moves out on the dusty plain, it means danger. Immediately you light a beacon fire – one column of smoke (or flame by night) for up to 500 raiders sighted, two for up to 3,000 and three for more than that. From beacon to beacon, the signal passes swiftly to the next garrison to summon help.

ABSOLUTE OBEDIENCE
An officer who killed two enemies without waiting for his orders was executed.

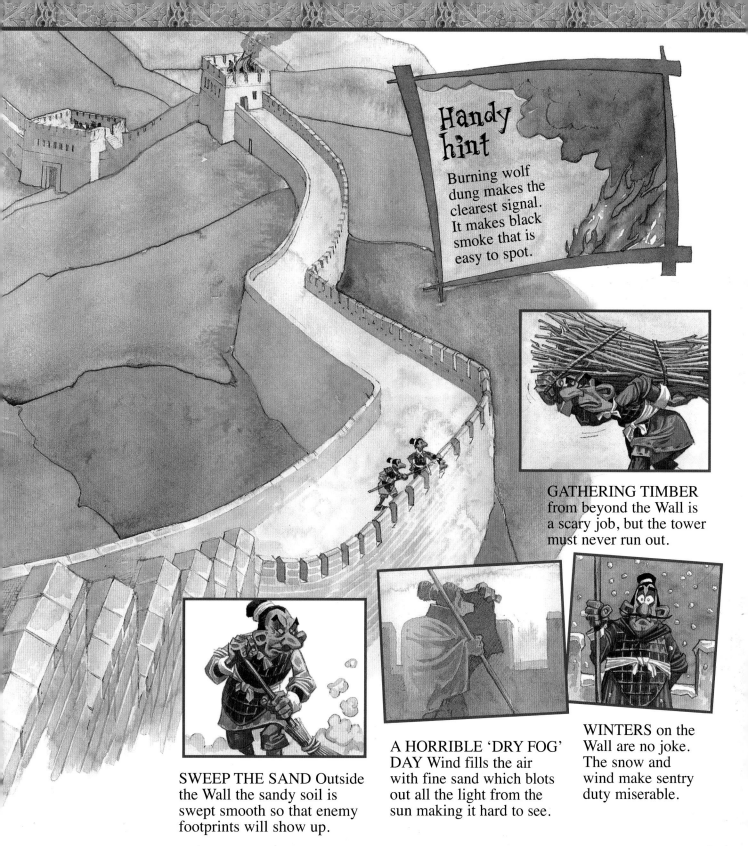

Handy hint

Burning wolf dung makes the clearest signal. It makes black smoke that is easy to spot.

GATHERING TIMBER from beyond the Wall is a scary job, but the tower must never run out.

SWEEP THE SAND Outside the Wall the sandy soil is swept smooth so that enemy footprints will show up.

A HORRIBLE 'DRY FOG' DAY Wind fills the air with fine sand which blots out all the light from the sun making it hard to see.

WINTERS on the Wall are no joke. The snow and wind make sentry duty miserable.

Guarding a gate

Day to day:

POSTAL SERVICE: You take letters to the next postal station along the Wall.

GOTCHA! You've caught an army deserter (left) who was trying to slip through the gate.

You've been transferred to a large garrison that guards a gate. It's the military headquarters for this stretch of the Wall, and its general has 100,000 men under his command. There has to be a gate in the Wall wherever it crosses a route used by travelling merchants from either side of the border. This means that when you're on gate duty it's your job to police it. You check passports, search wagons for goods being smuggled in, and watch out for illegal immigrants and criminals on the run.

CHECKING WAGONS (above left): He says it's only firewood underneath that cover, but is it?

MENDING THE WALL: Your section includes some older wall that's starting to crumble.

ALARM! Raiders have been sighted! You all grab weapons and rush into line.

INSPECTION: You dread the general spotting something about you that's not perfect.

A Lifetime by the Wall

Time passes. You hear that the Emperor has died and after a violent revolution, a former rebel is now Emperor. But all this matters little to you. You've finished your army service but you're stranded here, without the money or the permit to make the long journey home. Your father is dead, your farm is sold, and your sister is married and part of another family. There's no choice but to make your home here in northernmost China, with its hot summers, freezing winters, and hard, dry soil. It's government policy to settle people here to protect the border and to grow food for the army. You've been granted land, you've married a local girl, and you're farming again – but you're facing a lifetime by the Wall.

"FIND ME THE ISLAND of the Immortals," the Emperor ordered, desperate to escape death. But his efforts were in vain.

HE DIED unexpectedly on a tour of eastern China. Plotting to seize power, the ministers with him tried to conceal his death. The Emperor travelled in a covered chariot, but his body started to smell. To hide this, they put a cart of rotting fish behind the chariot.

Handy hint

If the Emperor sends you on an impossible mission, it's best not to return.

HEARING THE Emperor was dead, his long-oppressed people started a revolt, led by a labourer facing execution.

THE REBELS TAKE OVER The capital burned for three months, and soon after the entire Qin family were dead.

Glossary

Beacon A signal given by lighting a fire.

Branded To burn someone with a mark as a punishment and to show they have done something wrong.

Commute To change a punishment into a lighter one.

Confucius A Chinese thinker who is still highly respected for his wisdom.

Conscription officer An official with the power to force people to join the army or the public workforce.

Crossbowman An archer armed with a bow that fires mechanically propelled arrows.

Elixir of life A magical drink or mixture that would prolong someone's life forever.

Fortifications Walls, towers and other structures designed to keep an enemy out.

Garrison A large number of soldiers stationed in one place in order to defend it.

Hemp A coarse fabric woven from the fibres of the cannabis plant.

Hornet A large and aggressive insect of the wasp family.

Immigrants Foreigners entering a country with the hope of living there.

Jackal A wild member of the same animal family as dogs.

Permit Official written permission to do something.

Quicksilver Another name for Mercury, a silvery metal that is always in a liquid form.

Qin Pronounced 'chin.' The Chinese state that conquered all the others and the origin of the modern name 'China.'

Quota The amount of something, that is alotted to a person.

Soothsaying Foretelling the future often with the use of magical objects.

Steppes Vast, treeless plainlands.

Superstitious Strongly believing that magic and luck affect everyday life.

Terracotta A reddish clay often used in making pots.

Index